FIVE LAWS THAT GOVERN PRAYER

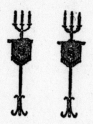

FIVE LAWS THAT GOVERN PRAYER

By

S. D. GORDON
Author of "Quiet Talks" Series

Five Addresses
Delivered at the School of Foreign Missions,
Woman's Foreign Missionary Society,
Methodist Episcopal Church,
at Lakeside, Ohio

NEW YORK   CHICAGO

Fleming H. Revell Company

LONDON   AND   EDINBURGH

New York: 158 Fifth Avenue
Chicago: 17 North Wabash Ave.
London: 21 Paternoster Square
Edinburgh: 75 Princes Street

6 3 5 8

CONTENTS

I

INTRODUCTORY

The Five Laws

A LAW is a habit of action, or, as the men with big words say, it is the sequence of events. There is a habit in all life. In the natural world the habit of gravitation we call the *law* of gravitation. And so in the human world, and in the spirit-life, there are laws that govern the practice of prayer.

I want to name five laws, as simple as the law of gravitation in the natural world, five laws that govern the use or practice of the habit of prayer. They are—the Law of Need, the Law of Abiding, the Law of the Use of Jesus' Name, the Law of Skill or Practice, and the Twin-Law of Confidence-Persistence. These are the five laws that underpin all prayer, whether simple or skilled.

The Law of Need is the basal law. It is always need that drives one to his knees. Everybody must confess this law. When

7

need comes, no matter who, or where, or what we are, we find ourselves pulled to our knees.

The Law of Abiding is the law of relationship. It is the touch between the man who prays and the One to whom he prays.

The Law of the Use of Jesus' Name is the foundation of all. We cannot do anything except we come in the Name of the distinctive, solitary God-Man who died as nobody ever died, or could, or can die.

Then there is the Law of Practice or Skill. A child can pray. A drunken man may come, and pray, and be heard, if he wants to be. And, then, prayer is the finest of fine arts. It is an art of the heart. And nobody ever gets to the place where he cannot learn a bit more about how to pray so as to change things that need changing.

The fifth Law is in one's spirit, Confidence-Persistence. You are persistent because you are confident; if you are persistent it is because you are confident. The two go together. We commonly say faith. That simply means that you know the thing you ask for is coming; that it is as sure as that Jesus died, and lived again afterward. And being so sure, you simply hang on. You have not the least idea of stopping; you insist and persist, and go a bit longer, seven times, seventy times seven, and then a bit more mathematics on the basis of seven, if need be. Then you quit counting. You simply persist until the answer comes. And your confidence is that the answer will come. And the answer does come.

I

THE FACT OF PRAYER

I

THE FACT OF PRAYER

Illustrating the Laws of Need, of Abiding, and of Confidence-Persistence [1]

THIS talk is to be on *the fact of prayer*. Prayer is a fact. You could say it is a talk on the Law of Confidence-Persistence. It is both. The sun is a fact. Prayer is a fact. You may question it. So much the worse for you, if you have not more sense. But a fact never changes because of your questioning.

Prayer takes three organs of the face or the head: an ear and a tongue and an eye. First the ear to hear; then the tongue to repeat the Master's promise; and then the looking-out, simply, steadily, expectantly, until the result comes. Bible reading is the listening side of prayer.

Prayer changes things. It changes things at the other end. It changes things at this end—

[1] Throughout these addresses, the style of the direct spoken word has been preserved on the printed page.

the praying end. When prayer can make any change it likes at the praying end, it will make any change you like at the other end. When God can reach in His hand and do as He likes with us, we can reach out our hands and do as we like with—God.

You think that is putting it pretty stiff. "Do as we like with God!" That sounds almost irreverent. Well, if you are thinking that way, go off in a quiet corner where it is quiet enough to think, and examine the first half of the sentence, for without any doubt the edge of the knife is in the part nearest yourself. If you can stand the tug on your life of the first half of the sentence you will have no bother about the second half. But if you balk on the first, that is the end of the book of that experience for you.

This talk is very simple—no theory, no argument, no philosophizing, just two bits out of life. I speak of them positively because I know them both personally. One bit from this side of the salt water, one bit from the other side.

One afternoon in a little suburb of old London, a lady spoke to me at a drawing-room meeting. She had been reading a little book

that said that prayer would change things.
And she said, " I believed that, but I wondered if it were true." She had been taught
the theory; would it work out in her case?

Then she told me what she was thinking
about. She had a brother in Calcutta who was
not a Christian. It is always some *one*. He
laughed at her Christian faith. She had
prayed, and no change had come. And she
had lost heart. Unconsciously she had lost
faith. Without knowing it she had lost the
prayer out of prayer; the words remained, the
thing itself was gone.

Then there was a bit of fresh touch with the
Man that died. And a bit of new, simple
prayer began that a man's will in Calcutta
might change, and change from the inside—the
only decent way a will can change. In the
course of her letter-writing to her brother, she
put in this question, " Has anything unusual
happened to you lately? "

When the answer came back it spoke of the
usual matters of family correspondence. And
then he said: " You asked if anything unusual
had happened lately. Yes, something has. On
such and such a day [naming the day] I began thinking about God. I don't know why.

It wasn't any book I was reading. It wasn't any service I was attending. But I knew my heart was not pure, and I knew my life was not straight. I tried to push the whole thing away, but it would not push. It stayed, and it stuck. And so I got out mother's copy of the Bible from the bottom of my trunk, and I got down on my knees, and I took mother's Saviour as my Saviour. And this is what has happened. I have become a Christian."

And I wonder if you can feel how she felt as she thought quickly back, and knew that the date named in his letter was the date when she began her new bit of praying in London. Prayer changes things. It changes things at the other end. It changes things at this end, the praying end. When prayer can make any change it likes at the starting end it will make any change you like at the other end.

The second bit out of life is from this side of the salt water. I got it from the man directly concerned. He was born in Maine. He was college bred. He was bred to the law. He was a giant in physique and in leadership among his fellows, and he was a skeptic. He used to lecture with great eloquence against the mere existence of a God. In the course of events he went to the Mississippi Valley to pursue the practice of law, and then a bit later he was sent to Washington to represent his district in the Lower House of Congress.

He said to me: " I was sitting at my desk in the Lower House listening to the very exciting debate as to whether Rutherford B. Hayes, of Ohio, or Samuel J. Tilden, of New York, should sit in the White House for four years. Not a time to think about your soul," he added with a smile. " I was listening keenly when there came to me a distinct impression that God was just there, (indicating with his out-stretched hand) and that He was looking at me, and that He was displeased with my attitude toward Himself."

He said to himself, " This is ridiculous. I am getting morbid. I have been working too hard. I will go and have a long walk in the fresh air, and a good meal at the hotel, and get rid of this absurd impression."

And he had a long walk through the park along the Potomac, and a well-ordered meal, and he came back to his seat. And he said to me, slowly, impressively, " Mr. Gordon, so did the impression come back—God just there, looking at me, and so on. And that thing went on day by day for some weeks. But nothing more took place at that time."

Then he had occasion to return to his home in the Central West. And he told me he was planning to get the nomination of his political party for the governorship of his state. And in that state a nomination by that party was, and is, practically equivalent to an election.

" The greetings were over with my wife," he said, " and I was quietly resting, when she said in a very tactful way, ' Henry, two of us have made a covenant of prayer that you shall become a Christian, and become the real kind.' "

Instantly he thought about that strange experience in Washington. But he did not want his wife to know how concerned he was, so assuming an indifference he did not feel, he asked her when " this prayin' thing " began. She named the date.

And he said to me, " I did some pretty quick thinking, and I knew in a moment that she had named the date when the impression came to me for the first time. And I was tremendously shaken. I was honest; I believed there was no God. But I was a lawyer, and used to sifting evidence, and here was a bit of evidence.

When those two women did something that they called praying, on the banks of the Mississippi, something akin to that happened to me two thousand miles away." And he softened his voice and said, " I think if somebody had just known how to take me I think I might have made the great surrender that very night."

But the next night he went with his wife to the Methodist church where she had her membership. And at the close of the service, when the opportunity was given, he rose to his full height, and walked down the aisle, the hardest walk he ever took, from one angle. Every step was breaking a precedent, a serious thing for a lawyer to do. Every step said, " I have been wrong." But he walked down deliberately, and knelt at the altar, and made the simple surrender of his strong will to the Higher Will.

And then an old boyhood conviction, from the early Maine days, came back to him, and he said, " I knew that I was to spend my strength, not in law, not in Congress, not in the governorship, but in pleading the case of one Client with my fellow-men. And as I knelt there I accepted the retainer for the rest of my life, and the rest of my strength." And as he rose from the altar and went back to his seat the whole course of his strong life was radically reversed.

Then one evening I had gone into their home for a bit of tea, and a bit of fellowship of spirit. After eating, I said to the wife, " Would you tell me your side of this thing? " And this, in effect, is her story: They were having some meetings in her church. And she had gone to the altar and knelt, and had a fresh touch with Jesus. There were some things in her life that were not wrong, but they were not the best, so they went out.

The real Jesus-man does not live on the level of putting the wrong out and the right in. He lives up on this level,—what would please my Master? So there was the fresh touch, and then the old time desire for her husband came back with fresh intensity. And she began thinking and praying. She found by her side a dear woman-friend kneeling likewise. And they made a covenant of prayer that day by day they would pray that this man might come to Christ.

That night the wife knelt by her bedside with her usual petitions. And then she came to this special petition. And she thought of her friend likewise praying. And then she began her prayer. And as she was praying very earnestly for her husband, she heard an inner voice, very quiet, saying, " Are you willing for the results? "

That startled her a bit; she was not used to a voice seeming to really speak to her. So she ignored the voice and went on praying. A second time, very quietly, the inner voice said, "Are you willing for the results? " And again she pushed the voice aside. And a third time, soft as the dews of Hermon, clear as the vibrant notes of a bell, quiet as only he knows who has heard the voice, came the words, " Are you willing for the results? "

And now she seemed to understand. So she said, " Lord Jesus, I am willing for any results You think good to come if only Henry may be out-and-out for You." And she told me that the sweetest peace came into her heart. She went on praying day after day for several weeks. But all the time there was the settled conviction that Henry was coming. And so he was. And so he did. And he came all the way. And he stayed where he came.

What were the results with her? She was

the wife of a lawyer with a large practice, and a large income. She was the wife of the congressman of her district. She would likely have been the wife of the governor of her state, and the first lady socially of the capital city.

She became a Methodist preacher's wife, with a very different income, and a very different social status as the world reckons social status. And yet I have never met a woman anywhere in the five continents who had in her face more of that fine beauty that comes only when the peace of God is regnant in the heart.

Prayer changes things. It changes things at the other end. It changes things at this end, the praying end. When prayer can make any change it likes at the starting end, it will make any change you like at the other end. When our Lord Jesus can reach in His pierced hand— and it is a grasping hand, too, a hand of power in changing, a hand of power in taking; aye, he has a sweep to Him, this Jesus. . . .

When He can gently, quietly, decisively, radically do as He likes in you and me, we can reach out our eager, longing hand and do as we like with Jesus, and among men, and in the circumstances of life. If you will stand the tug of the first half of that sentence, you will have no bother about the second half. You will have the organ stops all out, and the songs all ringing, because of victory coming, and because of victory present in your life and circumstances.

I told this story one morning at a laymen's missionary convention in Cincinnati a number of years ago, where two thousand business and professional men had paid a dollar apiece to get in. As I turned to my seat the presiding officer called on the song leader to sing a solo. And I could see out of the corner of my eye that he was shaking his head sidewise, declining to sing.

After the benediction I saw him coming toward me. Then I knew why he had not sung. The man was too full to sing. Under a fine self-control there was clearly an emotional upset within. He gripped my hand hard and said, " Gordon, was that Henry Otis Pratt you were telling us about?" "Why, yes," I said; " do you know Dr. Pratt?" "Yes," he said; " I know him very well." And then the eye flushed, and with a moment's pause for control, he said very quietly, " The other woman in that covenant of prayer was *my mother!*"

And that personal touch seemed to put the touch of the real on the whole thing. Ah, God is real. The Old Book is real. Jesus is real. Prayer is real. If—you have to stick in the *if*—if only *we* were real in letting Jesus have sweep and sway ——!

II
HINDRANCES

II

HINDRANCES

Illustrating the Law of Abiding

PRAYER fails sometimes. Prayer fails oftentimes. But the failure does not affect the fact of prayer, nor the principle of prayer, by so much as the half-batting of your eyelid.

Does your clock ever stop? Does it ever run slow, or fast? Of course. It fails you. It fails to tell the time, or to tell the accurate time. But the failure does not affect the fact of the clock, nor the principle of the clock. You still run your affairs pretty much by the clock on the mantel, or the pocket-clock in your clothes.

Now prayer fails. There is no question whatever about that. There are countless numbers of prayers that go out and bring nothing in, that go up and bring nothing down. This is quite clear. Prayer is often a clean, clear, sheer, dead failure.

But the failure does not affect the principle of prayer, or the fact of it, not by as much as

27

the third of the width of a narrow hair. Indeed, oftentimes the failure is a tribute to the power of prayer. It reveals somebody behind the scene—unseen—who believes so thoroughly in the power of prayer, and has reason to know its power against himself, that he is doing his level best, and then his level best heaped-up, to make the thing fail.

It is a small thing, you know, that your prayer fails. " Oh," you say, " you don't mean that; a small thing that my prayer fails! It is everything to me." Yes, everything to you, but it is a small thing, in contrast, with the heart-breaking thing that God's plan, God's purpose of prayer, is failing so much throughout the whole Church of Christ in all the six continents to-day.

In the old Book of God there are three things spoken of that hinder God's plan of prayer. First of all, anything in us that breaks off connection with God. If the connection is broken the current cannot get through. And this explains great numbers of unanswered, useless prayers.

And then there may be good connection, and yet a lack of skill in praying, a failure to fit in with the law of practiced skill in prayer. You

say, "Yes, that's the bother; I have no skill."
Go slow there; don't climb behind that fence
to hide yourself. Because it is skill of the
heart. And it comes easily, and not slowly, to
the one who is *willing* to have skill.

Then there is a third thing that hinders
God's plan of prayer. It is something that is
not talked about much, and not believed in
much by some good folk. It is this: Satan has
the power to hold the answer back for a while.
He does not have power to hold it back ulti-
mately and finally. But he *does* have the
power to check and choke and becloud and
hinder for a while. And the devil has rather
a free hand with some dear folk.

But all truth is dual, two-sided. And here
is the other side of that truth. Prayer in
Jesus' Name—pleading His Name, His power,
His blood—completely cuts the ground from
under the evil one's feet. Satan has the power
to hinder prayer for a time, *but* prayer, by
somebody in touch of heart with Jesus, defeats
the evil one. And the answer comes as surely
as that Jesus left Joseph's tomb clean empty
on the morning of His resurrection.

I want, here, to say a very simple bit about
the first of these hindrances, the things in us

that hinder God's plan of prayer. I am really talking on the second of the laws of prayer named in the last chapter—the Law of Abiding. The basis of prayer on our side is abiding. This bit touches the negative side of the Law of Abiding, the failure to abide. The other side of abiding is breaking. And there are a great many folks who are blessedly saved, and yet they are breaking with Christ all the time.

Here again there is a dropping into three groups. The first thing I would name that hinders prayer is sin, S-I-N. If I regard sin in my heart the Lord will not hear, which means in this case *cannot* hear. The connection is broken.

There is nothing surprising about this, of course. It is very commonplace. You see, sin is slapping God in the face. It may be cultured sin. Sin can take on a very high polish. Isn't it queer how coarse things can take a high polish? Or it may be just the common gutter-stuff that we cultured folk think ourselves above and turn away from. But whether coarse or cultured, sin is slapping God in the face. How can He and I do business together if I am treating Him like this?

If I had a private wire from this place to my home in New York City, and somebody should go out and cut the wire, even a child knows that I cannot telegraph over that wire. The ends are not a mile apart, not a yard apart, but just distinctly apart. Yet I might sit in my room, and tick away and use the most beautiful language. What's the use? The wire is cut. All my nice talk goes into the air or into the ground.

Now sin cuts the wire between us and God. "Well," somebody may say, "now you are cutting us all out, aren't you?" You say, "Isn't it true that we are all sinners, more or less?"

It certainly is true that the nearer you get to Jesus, and the more you get of victory in your life by the Holy Spirit's touch and presence and power, and the more you know of the power of the blood of Jesus in your daily life, the more conscious you are of a something inside there tugging down, and to be victoried over. You never are free of the sense of that power that tugs down, even when victory is flooding your life every waking and sleeping hour.

But, what the Old Book here plainly means is this: If I hold in my life something that

Jesus does not like, whether it be something that is wrong in itself, or something that the quiet voice has told me directly, or through the Book, Jesus does not like, that to me is sin. That is a breaking of the Law of Abiding, and I had better quit praying, and get things straightened out, because my prayer is a useless waste of breath. And it is a deceptive thing, for I may say, "I am not as good as you, I know I am not as good as I ought to be, but, still, I pray."

Sin is busy to-day, with a sharp-edged knife, cutting the nerve of countless prayers. And yet there need not be any morbid introspection, or unhealthy raking-over of the coals of your motives all the time. (But I need not caution you about that, for that is not the prevailing sin just now.) Jesus knows if the passion of my heart is to please Him. He understands, and I do. And when the passion of my heart is to please Jesus, that sweeps all the decks clear. The door is set wide open. And the prayer answers come in with a flood-tide beyond measurement.

Then a second thing that hinders prayer is spoken of by James in his little letter. He says, "Ye ask and receive not——" This is a pretty old affair. It bothered them in the first century—away back at the heart of things in Jerusalem. " Because ye ask amiss to use it on your pleasures." That is to say, You ask selfishly for something, just because you want it for yourself, regardless of anything else.

Take a very homely illustration: Here is a mother praying for her boy. He is a good boy, but not a Christian by his own outer action. She is thinking to herself, " I don't want my boy to be a prodigal. He bears our honored family name. I want him to grow up an honor to his father, myself and our family. And if he is a real Christian he very likely will."

And so she prays that he may be a Christian. And the prayer is answered. The Spirit touches the boy's heart. He opens the door, and the change takes place on the inside.

Then the new Master says to the boy, " My boy, I would like to have you give Me the use of your life to tell the folks in Africa that I died for them." And the boy, in the fine flush of his love, says, " Yes, Master, thank you, I am so glad to go."

But the mother! Oh! she never meant that. Her boy a preacher, a missionary, and, of all places, among the blacks of Africa! She meant him to be just a fine Christian gentleman at home, near by. The prayer itself is wholly good. The motive underneath is uglily selfish.

The stream of the mother's life is turning in. And when all the streams turn in, that means a Dead Sea. And I am afraid a great many dear, cultured, lovely, Christian folk have lives like the boundary line of the Dead Sea. All the streams turn in, with an occasional trickling out permitted for good observation purposes.

And without doubt this explains countless unanswered prayers. The Law of Abiding turns into a law of breaking. And yet again, there need not be any unwholesome raking-over of the coals of our motives. Jesus knows if the passion of my heart is to please Him, the passion that burns like an anthracite fire consuming all else as dross. We may be led to ask for a great many personal things, and even extras. Yes, He will give you quail in the desert. That is an extra on the bill of fare. But under all is the passion to please Him constantly sifting the praying.

Then the Old Book speaks of a third thing that hinders prayer. I hesitate to speak of it

because it is so very common. Will you listen
softly? *An unforgiving spirit* cuts the nerve of
prayer. Have you noticed how Jesus talks
about forgiveness *and* prayer? I used to
wonder why He coupled the two so much, but
I don't wonder so much now. It is quite clear
to me now. Everywhere, this difficulty sticks
out.

In the eighteenth chapter of Matthew Jesus
is talking about prayer, and Peter seems to
remember the remark about prayer and forgiveness. And so Peter asks a question. " Master," he says, " how many times must I forgive
a man? seven times? "

Clearly Peter is thinking that he is growing
in grace; he can actually think now of forgiv-
ing one man seven times straight away. He is
leaving the rounds of the ladder behind him
surely in the upper climb, Peter *thinks*.

And our Lord says, in effect, " Peter, you
have not caught the idea. Forgiveness is not a
question of arithmetic. It is not keeping tab on
your neighbor. Not seven times, but seventy
times seven." And the Luke account says
" in one day."

Plainly, our Lord is thinking that Peter will
lose count, or get tired of counting. Or, what

He really means, of course, is that he will breathe in the spirit of forgiveness.

And then our Lord, as He was so fond of doing, tells a story to illustrate His meaning. Here was a man who owed his lord a thousand talents. The real meaning here is about ten billion dollars—an amount too big to pay. And this man went to his lord and said, " I am a bit short. I cannot quite square the account. But I mean to pay, and I will if you will be easy with me." And his lord generously forgave him the whole debt. That is Jesus' picture of God who knows God best.

Then this man goes out and finds a fellow-servant who owes *him* something. Surely Jesus had a sense of the ludicrous, for it is shown here. The fellow-servant owed about sixteen dollars and a few red coppers over! That is the comparison. And the debtor who had been forgiven his vast debt took the other by the throat and said, " Pay up what thou owest."

The condition of the man's throat was not quite conducive to free speech. But he said as best he could, " I am a bit short. I cannot quite square the account. But I mean to pay. And I will if you will be easy with me." You would think the words would have sounded familiar. But he would not. He put him in the jail, the last place to pay a debt, but the old-fashioned way. That is Jesus' picture of man who knows man best.

And, in effect, our Lord says, " What you and I have been forgiven is like ten billions of dollars, something we cannot begin to pay. *And* what we cannot quite forgive that old neighbor or acquaintance or kinsman, is like sixteen dollars and sixty-six red copper cents, by comparison! " How small sin *can* shrivel a man up to be! And Jesus says, in effect, " You must forgive freely, gladly, graciously, generously, if you are to pray."

Somebody will say, " Oh, you don't know how hard it is to forgive." No, I don't know much. But I know two things: I have discovered in the first place that there are some things, and some folks, one cannot forgive of himself. I have discovered that.

And then I am very grateful to say that I have made a second discovery. Will you listen softly? When the Holy Spirit is allowed full sway of the heart He will make you love the man you can't like. He will make you love the man you don't like, with a real, warm, tender

love in your heart that will make you go out
of your way and sacrifice to help him. But we
must forgive if we are to pray. It is the Law
of Abiding. It is the law of not breaking
contact.

Now, please notice keenly here—it is *not* as
though Jesus would say to one, " There is sin
in you, go away; I will not have anything to
do with you." And to another, " You are
selfish, get out of My sight." And again,
" You have a bitter feeling in your heart."

It is not that at all. Just the reverse. Sin,
selfishness, hard feelings, those are Satan's
wide-open doors into a man's life. And he
has never yet been known to fail to use any
open door. He comes in and queers our Lord's
whole plan of prayer. And—this is hard to
say, but it is true—the evil one has a wide-
open door, and free sway, and he is spoiling
the whole plan of God, in the life of many a
Christian to-day. It is evident to us all, if we
but think.

If only we might repeat those words of
Jesus, on the night of the betrayal, when He
said, " The prince of this world cometh and he
hath nothing in me." Without doubt Jesus
was the only one who could ever say that, as

He said it, in the achievement of His life, as well as in the purpose of His heart.

But we *can* say this: Though the prince of this world comes—he is all the time coming, subtly, stormily, with Christian phraseology and veneering—he shall have nothing in me, no coaling station on the shore of my life; but Jesus, the scarred, the Calvary-Man, the victorious Third-Morning-After-Man, Jesus shall have full sweep and sway.

Then the Law of Abiding is fixed tight. You may ask what you will. The fences are all down now. Ask what you will, and the answer will come. There may be a bit of waiting-time, for prayer is a spirit-conflict. But as sure as Jesus died and rose again the floodtide of answer will come rushing into all the channels of your life.

III

FOUR OLD PICTURES

Illustrating the Law of Practiced Skill

HAVE you ever seen a little baby, just learning to toddle, reaching out for a bright red apple in the mother's hand? The baby's eyes are all aglow, its face all a-beam with eagerness and expectancy.

But the baby's muscles and the baby's eye have not yet been trained to work together, and so the little one's hand slips off to this side and misses the apple, and slips off that side and misses the apple, and maybe falls short in another attempt.

And then the baby's face clouds. Local showers threaten. Then the mother croons and woos. And the baby tries again. And by and by the little fat chubby fingers are holding as tight to the bright red apple as only baby fingers can hold. Have you ever seen that?

" A little child shall lead them." This little child may teach us a lesson. The child is thinking about the bright red apple, and nothing else. The mother is thinking about the apple too.

She wants her baby to have it. But the mother's thought has gone a bit farther. She is thinking of her baby, of the training of muscle and eye together. And so there is a waiting time. It seems pretty serious to the baby.

And some of us are just babies grown a bit older, and things look mighty serious when the hand does not touch the apple. Of course, the mother could instantly put the apple over into the child's hand, and the child would have all that it wants. But the mother wants more. And so there is a waiting time.

It is a good deal like that in prayer. Prayer is a fine art, although one remembers that it is an art of the heart. A little child may come and pray. The immature Christian may come and pray. The man just repenting of his sins, in the dirt of his life, may come and pray and be heard. And the man of finest culture and deepest consecration and longest years of spiritual experience finds that prayer as a fine art swings into action all the powers of life and years and experience.

Just here I want to add a very simple word about the Law of Practiced Skill in praying. We learn best by stories and pictures. A story is a picture for your ear. A picture is a story for the eye. The Old Book teaches largely by stories and pictures. The Older Testament is the picture-book, the Newer leaves are the teaching-book. And it is very interesting to note that for every bit of teaching in the New there is a story or picture in the Old, and for every picture or story in the Old there is a bit of teaching in the New.

It is one Book from end to end. It is not bad to remember *that*, in *our* day. The two parts of it are like the two parts of a pair of scissors held together by a rivet. You have to have both sides of a pair of scissors in action to get a clear cut. You have to have both sides of the Old Book in action to get a clear cut into the fabric of any truth of God's Word.

It is one Book throughout, with the same standard of morals throughout, the same tender love, and the same high ideals. Of course a Man comes in the newer part. All the colorful personality of a Man, the God-Man walking amongst us, in human guise, gives an intensity to it. But it is the same thing throughout, with that personal climax in the New.

I want to touch on four stories out of life that illustrate the Law of Skill and Practice in prayer. They bring to us, in a word, the difference between the child's reaching hand and the mother's reaching hand. And the whole thing in prayer and in the skill of prayer is getting the hands together. Because no human hand has ever yet reached up, to take as much as the Pierced Hand is reaching down to give. That is the pathos of it. God cannot get folks anywhere who will reach up and out and take all He is reaching down eagerly to give.

Four stories: the story of Moses' prayer to go into the Promised Land, and God said, " No "; the story of Hannah's prayer for a son, and the answer delayed for years; then, changing the chronological order, Paul's thorn; and, finally, Jesus' changed prayer in Gethsemane. I put the four together, purposely, so that we may have all four together in our thinking.

First, the Moses story: Moses is a giant from any standpoint. Lawgiver, cultured, scholarly, with the rarest learning of the rarest scholarly center of all the world in his day, a general and an organizer, an orator—he is the great racial giant among those who are men only. He said that all he did was the result of prayer. He asked. God did. He reached out and took what God was reaching down to give. His story, throughout, is simply a story of asking, and of answered prayer.

There is one exception. There is a reason. God is never capricious. He is the most sweetly reasonable Being in all this world of ours. The facts are these: The people are in the wilderness, it is a new life, a difficult life, bristling with difficulties and questions. The people have no water. That is serious, not to have water, three or four million of them, with the babies and growing children and stock— very serious. No; it *was* not serious at all, because God was along, and this whole journey was God's affair. But the people forgot God. They had better stomachs than memories. They could remember the garlic and the leeks and the onions of Egypt, but they forgot God. They must have been kin to a few folks of our own time and years.

So they criticised. That's the easiest thing in the world to do. It takes less brains than anything else. Perhaps that is the reason it is so common. So they began to pick and nag at Moses. You brought us here to kill us all! And God said, " Moses, give them the water, they must have water." (Just like God, to

overlook the criticism!) "Speak to the rock,"
—it had been struck once—" I will give them
what they need."

But Moses had not reached either God's
level of patience—who has?—nor his own
later level of patience. Patience is the highest
accomplishment of human life. So here is the
picture of what the people saw. Moses with
eye flashing, hot bitter word on the tongue,
hard blow on the rock, "You rebels!" That
is what the people saw. They said, "That's
God." And they were hurt. We can easily
understand how they felt.

They were mature in body, but pretty much
children otherwise—like a few other folk. And
they looked up and said, "That is God!"
Poor God! slandered by Moses. But then that
is not the last time. Nobody so misunderstood
as God. And God said, "Something must be
done to tell these people that that is *not* what
I am like." For this was not *a* nation, it was
the messenger nation to work out God's plan
for *the race*.

Something must be done to teach the people
that that is not what God is like. So God said,
"Moses, you may not go into the Promised
Land, you have disobeyed Me. I told you to

speak; you struck.   Something must be done; you may not go into the Promised Land."

And Moses said, " Please, I want to go— with the eagerness of a child, perfectly proper eagerness—please."   It is hard to be dis- ciplined, and to have folks know you are being disciplined. That cuts a bit. The third time he asks. And God says, " Moses, don't speak to Me any more about this; this thing is fixed."

Plainly, judging from the whole story, God would have said, " Yes," for Moses personally. He would have been forgiven straight off. That is the whole story of his life. But for the people's sake, that they might be taught that that is not what God is like, " No " was said to Moses.

Moses felt it very keenly.   The people felt it. And yet the damnable badness of disobedience, of not doing as God wants, the necessity of simple, full, gracious, glad obedience, was burned into the heart of this messenger nation by this incident much more than by flaming, smoking mount, or by voice of God out of the mount.

And so over that story you put down this simple sentence: The prayer was denied *for the people's sake,* that they might be taught and trained for their racial service through the centuries. And nobody was so grateful for the negative as dear old Moses, as from the hills of God looking down and looking back he saw how much God's "No" to him meant to the people, and meant to God's plan for the race.

The second story is Hannah's prayer for a son. The facts are something like these: The Samuel story comes in the first of two bad sags-down which the saviour-nation had. The Elijah story fits into the second. The saviour-nation is being lost, going bad. The plan of God for the race, through the centuries, is in danger. The whole thing hinges there.

God wanted a leader. But there were no leaders. They are a bit scarce, sometimes, even yet. And there were no men to train for leadership. And there were no women through whom might come men to be trained for leadership. That is the lowest a people ever gets, when the women go bad. It is the highest that goes lowest.

Hannah has in her the making of a woman through whom may come the man to be trained for leadership in the saviour-nation of the race. But Hannah must be changed before she can

be used. Most folks must. Or shall I cut out
the word " most " ? Nobody likes the cutting
of the chisel's edge. And so the years go by,
and out of the years there comes a new woman.

The curse of Lamech was over her home;
there were two wives. Hannah is the favorite,
but has no child; the other wife has children.
Every Hebrew woman longed for a son, the
normal instinct of maternity was yet stronger
with the Hebrew than in others, because a
woman's son might be her nation's Messiah
and the race's saviour. But Hannah has no
son, and she prays. But the answer doesn't
come. And the other woman picks and nags
and teases. And Hannah wonders why the
answer does not come to her prayer.

Well, why? Hannah is like the baby reaching for the apple; God is like the mother holding the apple. Hannah sees that home, that
atmosphere, a childless bosom, a disappointed
heart; she wants a son. All is perfectly normal
and natural; all she is thinking of is a baby boy
to cuddle to her lonely breast.

Here is what God sees: a nation, no, *the*
nation, *the plan for the race* in danger. He
wants a leader. But there is no leader, no men
to train for leadership, no women to bring a

man to be trained for leadership. And so the years go. And Hannah is changed, her vision broadened, her will strong enough to bend to the higher will, a willingness that what was hers first by good right, her boy, should be hers only in a secondary way, and should be the nation's and God's first. That is the highest level a mother can reach.

And then Samuel was born. No; farther back yet, he was conceived in an atmosphere of strong, intelligent, understanding devotion to God and to God's purpose. And Samuel came to be the man that he was by reason of those pre-natal months. He was made the giant he came to be by the spirit of the woman that was bringing him into the world. And over that story you put this simple sentence: The answer to the prayer was delayed for years that *more might be given and gotten.* And nobody was so grateful as Hannah for the years of schooling and of waiting.

Then the third of these stories is Paul's thorn, or his prayer about his thorn. If you talk rather positively about prayer being answered, somebody always remembers Paul's thorn with a bit of a smile, as though that thorn rather helped out some theory of theirs.

Well, there is always a reason, and with God it is always the reason of a great, tender love.

First a word about Paul. Paul is a giant. You rightly put him alongside of Moses. His Hebrew breeding, his Greek culture, his broad discipline, his tremendous will, his sympathetic nature, his devotion to God, and then to Jesus when he came to know Him—what a giant Paul was!

But Paul had a weak spot. Say it very quietly, because where you speak of one weak spot in him, you may think quickly of a score in yourself. All Paul's journeys spell out his tremendous will. But, sometimes, this Hercules in his will was a bit set in his way. God had a hard time holding Paul to His plan of service. Paul had a plan or two of his own.

From the very first of that Damascus-road scene, when the voice and light came, the word to Paul was, "the Gentiles," the outside, the non-Jew, the racial world. That was to be his field of service. And he went, with all his splendid devotion and strength.

But all the time Paul was thinking to himself, "The Jerusalem Jews—let me at them— I know that crowd; I trained with them, and they know me. They have crucified Jesus, they have practically stoned the Holy Spirit in the person of Stephen, but I can get them."

And you can understand perfectly the good side of it. It would be strategic if he could really win them; the wide grasp of the thing is tremendous. But the Master had said, " the Gentiles." That was to be his service. And Paul underneath said: " I will go to the Gentiles, but let me get at the Jerusalem Jew crowd."

And the thing even went so far that one day in the holy precincts of the Temple in Jerusalem Paul was kneeling in prayer, and Jesus graciously gave him a vision. And He said, " I want you to go to the Gentiles." And then something very strange took place—yet not so very unusual—Paul began to explain to the Lord Jesus why he should go to the Jerusalem Jews.

This is surely carrying things to great lengths. After Foch has given orders for a movement to have an under officer begin to explain why the order should be changed! Yet that is the picture. And then the interview is abruptly closed by the Lord saying, " Depart from Jerusalem where you are just now, to the outer, non-Jewish world." That is Paul, a giant before whom one bows his head in reverence; and yet with a weak spot, a bit set in his way. Most folks are. It is heart-breaking to Jesus.

Then the thorn came. Nobody knows what it was; it does not matter a grot. It was something in his body affecting his health. He called it a thorn, a needle-pointed thorn, cutting, sticking. Ugh! how it hurt! He did not think much of it at first because there was Jesus to go to. He went, he asked; the thorn stayed. He went again. The thorn got sharper, and cut in deeper. A third time he goes, with what eagerness one can well understand.

Now, notice three things about the answer to his prayer. There *was* an answer. God answers the man, though He denies the prayer. He does not ignore Paul; God never ignores anybody. He talks it out with him. He will talk things out with you, if you will give Him your ears.

The second thing—what it was God said to Paul. One night, late, Paul was slowing down a bit. The crowds were gone, canvas stitching over for that day; he was in bed, tired. But sleep would not come because of the sticking thorn. And Paul wondered that the thorn had not been taken away.

He is lying there thinking, maybe just a bit restless, when an inner voice came, soft as the dews of Hermon. And the voice said, " Paul, I know about that thorn, and how it hurts; it hurts me too, it hurts me because it hurts you. Paul, I would be so glad to take the thorn away, but "—the voice softens—" it is a bit better to have the thorn stay because only so can I have the use of you in *my* plan of service for the world." And a hush comes over Paul's spirit. He knows how true it is. A man comes to know himself pretty well when he is away off alone in the dark.

And then as he is lying there quietly, hushed, the voice comes again. It's the third bit of answer to his prayer. Yet more quietly the inner voice says, " Paul, I will be so near you, you shall have such a simple wondrous experience of my presence, that you will clean forget the sticking thorn-point, even while it bores its sharp way into your living flesh."

And I see Paul one night in his own hired house in Rome. The crowd is gone. He is slowing down a bit. One arm is around young Timothy, the other is over on dear old Dr.

Luke. And as you listen in, you hear Paul
saying, "Do you know, dear friends, I would
not have missed the thorn "—his voice hoars-
ens a bit with emotion, and he is silent; a hush
comes over them, and then he goes quietly on—
" for *the glory-presence of Jesus that came
with it."*

And over that story you may put down this
sentence: The man was answered, the prayer
was denied for service' sake, for the sake of the
race through the centuries since. And yet I am
very clearly in the belief that Jesus still prefers
to take away the thorn, *if* He may have His
way in our lives.

The fourth of these stories is Jesus' changed
prayer in Gethsemane. How shall I talk about
Jesus? Son of God; Son of man; God the
Son; God a man; as really God as though not
human at all; as really human as though only
human. Here in Gethsemane the human part
stands out pathetically, tragic, tremendous.

On the morrow Jesus is to be—I will use
Paul's phrase—"made sin for us." He is to
be treated as sin deserves to be treated. I
don't take that in, but I can repeat the words,
and hush my heart in awe at the horror of the
thing.

Jesus goes in among the old gnarly olives, leaving eight of His disciples, and taking three with Him in His longing for fellowship. Then He goes in deeper, alone. Now He is on His knees, and now on His face. And the horror of death is in His spirit, the dust of death in His throat.

Calvary was fought out in Gethsemane; Gethsemane is the anticipation of Calvary. The battle of the morrow is fought out under the olive trees. It is the only explanation of Gethsemane and Calvary, the twin events.

Now a bit of a prayer reaches the ear. " O My Father, if it be possible, if there be some way whereby Thy plan for the world can work out without this awful horror of My being made reckoned sin, if there be some way ——" the possibility even yet clinging, of the plan working out without this horror for Him.

And the blood-drops come. Already the earth is beginning to feel the fertilizing of the blood of the Son of God. Then the angels come. And then a calmer mood asserts itself.

And this is the point just now, *the changed prayer*. " O My Father, since this cup, this experience, may not pass away from Me, since only through this for Me can Thy plan for the world work out, I yield to it. It does not matter about Me; Thy loving plan for the race, Thy will be done through this experience for Me."

The prayer is hammered out on the anvil of His knees. That was true even of Jesus. There alone there came to Him very clearly—I think it was always clear—a realization that only thus could the Father's plan for the race work out.

That was true of Him—the prayer hammered into shape on the anvil of His knee. How much more of us! If we might slip away into a quiet corner, with the old Book open, and the knee bent, and the will bent, until we come to see things through God's eye, and yield ourselves to God's plan. Then we will learn to pray. And nothing shall be held back.

" Into the woods my Master went,
    Clean forspent, forspent.
  Into the woods my Master came,
  Forspent with love and shame.
  But the olives they were not blind to Him;
  The little gray leaves were kind to Him;
  The thorn tree (with its pricking thorns) had
      a mind to Him
  When into the woods He came.

" Out of the woods my Master went,
    And He was *well content*.
  Out of the woods my Master came,
  Content with death and shame.
  When the death and shame would woo Him
      last
  From under the trees they drew Him last:
  'Twas on a tree they slew Him—last,
  When out of the woods He came."

IV

THE CONVERSION OF
LOVED ONES

IV

THE CONVERSION OF
LOVED ONES

*Illustrating the Laws of Need, of Abiding,
of Confidence-Persistence, and of the Use
of Jesus' Name*

THE heart of the world's life is its
literature. The heart of the world's
books is this old Book of God, utterly
distinct from all other books, in the touch of
God's hand upon it. And the heart of this
Book is the New Testament. The Old has a
promise; the New has a Personality. In the
Old a promise looks forward; in the New a
Man walks amongst us.

And the heart of the New Testament is the
Gospels. And the heart of the Gospels is
John's Gospel. The man who lived closest
brings us closest. And there is an inner heart
again in John's Gospel in chapters thirteen to
seventeen.

When the twelfth of John comes to its close
you hear a door slamming, with a hard, ugly
sound. It is the Jewish national door. But

another door opens, the inner heart door of this group of men who have opened their hearts' doors to Jesus. And now He opens His inner heart door to these men who have opened their heart doors to Him.

He really does not open His heart door in chapter thirteen until Judas goes out. Jesus did His best to keep Judas in, His level best, heaped-up, bubbling over. But if Judas stayed in something must go out of Judas. Judas would not let anything go out, so Judas himself went out. And it was certainly a black night for Judas when he went out, for him the blackest of all.

If some of you are thinking that the Master has not opened His inner heart-door to you as intimately as you wish He would, you might look around the corners of your house, the house of your life. Maybe some of Judas' old ragged shoes are off in some dark closet-corner. Judas simply stands for the old self-life. Judas would actually use Jesus—it makes you cringe to say it—to help out his own selfish purposes. And yet Judas is not so lonely. He has company.

When Judas goes out the Master begins talking. Now they leave the upper room, they are walking along the street of the city. The passover moon is shining down on the great brass vine of Herod's Temple, and the Master breaks the silence by saying, " I am the *real* vine; that thing there, so pretty, is only brass; no blood of the grape there."

And He goes on, " If ye abide in me, and my words abide in you, ye shall ask what ye will, and it shall be done unto you." There is not a word about God's will directly, though it is implied, of course. There is something about our wills. Under these circumstances, ask whatever *you* will to ask, and—putting it in a very homely way, but very accurately— " I will lay myself out to bring that thing to pass for you somehow, regardless of all opposition."

Can you assure the conversion of your loved ones by prayer, without any question? There is no question that sets more hearts to beating a bit faster than that question. Can you? And should you if you can? Is it fair? A man is set against being a Christian; his will is cross-grained to Christ. Let us say for the moment that in the thing called prayer you have a power to change it. Is it fair to use this strange power to work against a man's will, and change him against his will?

One week, in the noon-meeting in the old Bromfield Street Methodist Church in Boston, I was talking about prayer. And a lady whom I knew, a cultured woman of mature years, came to me at the close and said, "Mr. Gordon, I don't think we can pray like that." I had been talking rather positively.

"Why not?" I said, and I knew by the bit of flush in her face and a little tremble of her lip how deep the tides were running.

"Well," she said, "I have a brother and he laughs at my Christian faith. The wine-glass, the card-table, the race-track—that is his life. I think I would rather than anything else that my brother were a Christian. But I don't think I can pray positively for his conversion in the way you suggest, because man is a free agent, isn't he? And God won't do anything against a man's will, will He?"

Now I want to say to you what I said to my Boston friend that noontime. Man *is* a free agent (to use the old theological term) as far as God is concerned. He is the freest of all beings in the universe. The one thing God insists upon is that every man shall be utterly free to do, to choose, to act, as he will. God bends over backward in His insistence on that.

But as far as selfishness and prejudice and superstition, and this thing we call sin, and the devil, are concerned, man is the most enslaved agent on the old footstool. And the whole purpose of prayer is never to crowd a man. God never crowds a man. He woos. And He warns. But He leaves one free.

And the whole purpose in prayer is never to crowd a man's will, but to set a man free. It is to free his will of selfishness and prejudice. And then, with somebody praying, the whole probability to the point of moral certainty is this: the man will come a-running on his own feet, in his own shoes, gladly to Jesus. And he will thank you for the prayer that set his will free from its enslavements. The exceptions to that statement are so extremely rare that none of us may ever know of a case in a long lifetime.

And now I want to give you four bits of the Book on which the prayer for your loved one hinges, in which the prayer is rooted. Everything, you know, depends on the Book. God talks in the Book. There is a living Presence here. There is a Voice that comes in the Book, a Hand that reaches out, a throbbing Heart that beats. Everything roots in the Book. But you don't stop in the Book; you go through it to Him who comes through it to you.

The first bit is this: " If ye abide in me, and my words abide in you, ask whatsoever ye will, and it shall be done unto you " (John 15: 7). Abiding does not mean to hire a night's lodging. It does not mean a lumberman's shack, nor a miner's shanty. By contrast it means moving into a brownstone house to stay, with the title deed in your own name.

" If ye *abide* in me, and *my words* abide in you "—these words sway deep, you know, even as the fire sweeps and sways the dry kindling in the grate. If you can stand the tug of John fifteen, seven, you will have the organ stops out, and the music filling and flooding the air because of answered prayer, when the spirit conflict is all through. This bit is on our side who do the praying.

Then the second bit of the Book is God's side of the prayer. It is Second Peter, three, nine: " Not willing that any should perish." That is *His will* regarding James or Mary, or anybody you are thinking of just now. We are taught to pray, " Thy will be done." Here is

His will—" not willing that any should perish."
If any man ever goes out of this life, out and
down, he goes against God's will and his going
that way is heart-breaking to God. Yet the
man is utterly free to do as he will.

The third bit of the Book gives the *process*
by which the prayer works out. It is Second
Timothy, two, twenty-four to twenty-six. This
has been a bit puzzling for our scholarly
friends. Let me read it as it runs: " And the
Lord's servant must not strive, but be gentle
toward all, apt to teach, forbearing, in meekness correcting them that oppose themselves; if
peradventure God may give them repentance
unto the knowledge of the truth, and they may
recover themselves out of the snare of the devil,
having been taken captive by him unto his
will."

Now let me make a paraphrase, a translation
of the thought: The Lord's servant must not
strive, not argue, not discuss, but be gentle toward all. Gentleness is not weakness; gentleness is strength accommodating itself to one
who is less strong. The father walks along
with a little toddler by his side, and he accom-
modates his step to the little baby steps. That
is gentleness.

Gentle toward all, apt to teach, quick to put in the word that makes clear the thing that is troubling your loved one; forbearing, very patient; in meekness instructing them that oppose themselves. The man who is not a Christian is opposing himself. Instructing, giving light, that God may help them to a change of mind about Himself, and they who have been taken captive by the devil may recover themselves out of his snare. Pretty rough talk, isn't it? that your loved one is the devil's captive. That is the *process* by which the thing works out.

And then *the form of the prayer* is suggested in Matthew six, thirteen. The old reading says, "Deliver us from evil." The Revision puts in the word "one." "Deliver us from the evil one." When you dig underneath the word "deliver," you find that you might use the word "rescue" here very accurately. It is a picture of a man traveling on donkeyback perhaps, with his servant, through one of those narrow defiles or gullies of Palestine. And some robbers come and take the man, and begin to do him violence, to steal what he has, and maybe leave him half dead. And as they are making their attack here comes somebody over the hill. In that land you know the help always came from the hills. That is the basis of Psalm 121: " I will lift up mine eyes unto the hills." The rescuing party comes along, and they drive back the robbers, and rescue the man. That's the picture meaning of that word " deliver," rescue. Now our Lord Jesus puts that bit into the prayer. Rescue us from the evil one. It helps us to see why these words are a part of the prayer.

And the way the prayer works, putting these last two bits together, is simply this. You are in touch of heart with Jesus, of course. You and Jesus have an understanding. You are working partners. Whatever He wants you will do, whatever you want He will do. Now you are talking with your Friend and Partner and Saviour, God.

And you are thinking about Mary or Charles, and you say, " Deliver him, rescue him from the evil one, and work in him Thy will for him, (not willing that any should perish) by Thy power, to Thy glory. In Jesus' Name."

And then you always add a bit: " *I thank Thee* because Thou art Victor. I thank Thee that Charles will be saved—set free—and he will come of his own free choice, in the shoes of his own cobbling—the only right way—to the Man that died."

And now *the way the prayer works out in effect,* is this. Your prayer at once begins to affect the whole atmosphere and scene of this man's life for whom you are praying. Shall I say something that may hurt you a bit? It has pained my heart many a time. Your loved one who is not a Christian is under the power of the evil one. It is rather the proper thing to-day to think there is no evil one. But the simple truth is that that rare old, subtle, splendid evil prince is in control of that life.

Now what your prayer does is this: You step over on the battlefield of that man's life in your spirit, in your thought. Every man's life is a battlefield. If Satan is in possession Jesus is wooing. If Jesus is in possession Satan is besieging.

You step over on the battlefield, and you hold up the blood-red banner of Jesus, the Man that died—died not as an example of fine fighting simply, though that is in it as the small dust of the balance—as the Saviour whose sacrificial blood only can have power to clean up and clean out the stains.

You lift the blood-red banner of Jesus on

the battlefield of your loved one's life and Satan cannot stand that. He hates the blood. He fears it. He flees from it. Not till he must, though. If you waver a bit he is in, quicker than a flash. Subtle old fighter! You and I are no match for him when it comes to fighting. But if the man praying just holds steady, Jesus delivers from this subtle evil one. And he goes, reluctantly, as slowly as he may, angrily, *but he goes*.

But prayer is a conflict, a spirit-conflict. The evil one will hang on as long as he can. And if you lose faith a bit and lose heart, he will push his trench closer in. But if one holds steady, Satan leaves the man you are praying for—free! He must! Your loved one is rescued from that evil power and evil presence. And then, once free, that loved one of yours, made in God's image as every human is, will come a-singing to Jesus. His eye clears, his hearing becomes keen and accurate, and in coming to Jesus he will come to the one true, full human level of human life.

If we might go out to-day into some quiet corner, and give Jesus all afresh the full sweep and swing of our wills and our lives, and then have a bit of time with Him daily over the

Book so that He can teach us, and then, as He guides pray, no thing and no one can resist, or want to resist the power. Our loved ones will come to Jesus gladly, and then thank us for praying them through to the coming-point.

A good many years ago there lived in old London a woman who earned her livelihood by the wash-tub and the ironing-board. She had a son, John, who ran away to sea in his teens. She did not know where he was for years. People said John was guilty of about every sin in the calendar, and pretty much every crime.

But, of course, the mother prayed for her boy. The fragrant dew of mothers' prayers is what keeps life sweet a bit longer. And many a time the dew of this mother's eyes mingled with the suds, and many a time the dew of her eyes helped dampen the clothes for the pressing as she prayed for John.

And, of course, the prayer was heard. No real prayer ever slipped yet. It cannot slip, for Jesus and His blood are back of it. And John came, and he came all the way, and then he became a preacher for Jesus. And John Newton, the sailor-preacher, was the means of helping men by the thousand into touch with Jesus.

There was one man among the thousands

that John Newton touched—scholarly, cultured, refined—who felt that he did not need a Saviour. He would walk in as he was, like some of his kinsfolk on this side of the water. But John Newton was used to touch Thomas Scott's heart. And Thomas Scott came to Jesus and found the need of a Saviour and the Saviour for his need. And then Thomas Scott, by tongue and by pen, was the means of changing the lives of thousands.

And Thomas Scott touched a young fellow—dyspeptic, melancholy—who thought he was too bad for God to save, just the reverse of Scott. Thomas Scott was used to touch William Cowper's heart. And William Cowper came to Jesus, and he found out about the blood that cleanses, and he wrote a bit of a hymn that some folks don't like to-day. But "There is a Fountain Filled With Blood" has been used to swing men by the uncounted thousands into touch with the Man who shed the blood. And I believe I will keep that hymn in my list a bit longer.

And William Cowper touched a man, William Wilberforce, known as the Christian statesman of England, the man that touched the great middle classes of England for Christ, the man who struck the shackles from the limbs of thousands of British slaves, and through simple preaching of the old story of Jesus swung people of the great middle classes of England into touch with Jesus.

And Wilberforce, among many, touched a man who was a clergyman of the Established Church in one of the Channel Islands—Leigh Richmond—and he was changed. And Leigh Richmond knew the story of a young woman in an adjoining parish, whose father was a dairyman, a very simple-hearted young woman. But she knew the Gospel of Jesus and lived it in a very simple, true way. He learned her story, and he wrote it down in a little bit of a book called *The Dairyman's Daughter*.

I remember reading it as a boy, and wishing I could be a Christian like that, and thinking I could not be. That little book went into forty languages, a remarkable thing back there when translation was so much less than now, into kings' palaces and peasants' huts, and everywhere between. And wherever it went it burned its way like a bit of living flame into men's hearts, changing them as it went.

Would you trace that little series of concentric circles? Here is the little bit of book,

The Dairyman's Daughter, burning like a fire wherever it went, and going everywhere. Here is Leigh Richmond writing it down, having dipped his pen into his heart; and Wilberforce touching Richmond, and Cowper, Wilberforce, and Scott, Cowper, and Newton, Scott, and— hush your heart, take off your hats and your shoes, please, in reverence—an old woman, gray-haired, with bent back, stubby fingers, and furrowed cheek, bending over her wash-tub and ironing-board, mingling her tears with the suds *as she prayed for her boy, John!*

Ah! if something else slips, shall we give first time to prayer? Shall we put our lives into full fresh touch with the Man who died, and give Him free hand to do as He will? Then nothing will fail to yield to the power of your prayer. The hard heart will soften; the stubborn will will bend—bend from the *inside,* the only decent way for a will *to* bend; the path will straighten, the light will break in the darkness, the disease will yield to the new touch of life, the sob will yield to the song, and the conflict to the victor.

V

THE SCHOOL OF PRAYER

THE SCHOOL OF PRAYER

Illustrating the Laws of Abiding, of the Use of Jesus' Name, of Skill, and of Confidence-Persistence

THE whole purpose of prayer is to change things that need changing. Prayer does us good. There is a subjective side to prayer, without doubt; tremendous, quite beyond calculation. And prayer has an objective value also, which means simply that it changes things outside that need changing in other lives, and would not be changed otherwise.

Now for a simple bit of homely talk about how to pray so as to change things that need changing, how to make sure that they will be changed, and changed every time. There need be no bill of exceptions in this court of prayer.

I want to give you *four suggestions* about how to pray so as to change things that need changing; and then *three simple conditions* of making sure without exception that prayer will change things every time, even to the stubbornest thing there is in existence, even the thing that is hardest to change in all human life and that cannot be changed, and ought not to be changed, except from the inside, that is, a man's will. The great battle of life is in a man's will, God's battle and ours.

Four suggestions, then, very homely. First, *prayer needs time,* daily time, quiet time, time when you are not tired. You say, " When's that? " Well, when you are not too tired. Because a tired mind cannot take in. And the big part in praying is taking in, being yielded, being susceptible to Somebody you cannot see; and then the going out, and changing things outside.

We must not make rules for others. Every life is its own battlefield. And every man must make his own rules and fight his own fight. But if you can manage the fighting line so as to get the morning-hour quiet, with the door shut, yourself off alone, so much alone that you are not alone, that is victory. If you stumble there, it will be a tale more or less of defeat and discipline all along the time. Prayer needs time.

Then *prayer needs a place.* Oh, you can pray anywhere, on the train, in the trolley, nursing a baby, sweeping the floor, chopping a typewriter, measuring calico, dictating a letter —you can pray anywhere. But you are not likely to. You are very *un*likely to, unless you have been off in the quiet place alone with Jesus. Jesus said, "Enter into thine inner chamber."

And, humanly, Jesus was an Oriental, and the Orient has no privacy, characteristically. Yet He said, "Enter into thine inner chamber." We western-hemisphere folk seem to be turning Parisian—we are living out on the boulevards, on the crowded streets of life. All the privacy appears to be gone out of our lives —aye, and all the fragrance and all the power, too. If Jesus, humanly an Oriental, could say "inner chamber," we can *get* it. Although it is a fight to get it, I know.

What or where the place is, does not matter a grot. With some of us it must change frequently. With me it changes continually. It may be the corner of a cathedral or the corner of a kitchen. The kitchen may be just as good for this purpose as the cathedral. Indeed some kitchens I have known better than some cathedrals I have been in.

The thing is this: His presence, the presence of the Unseen but real Jesus. When you are alone, you are not alone. The more alone we are so far as men are concerned, the less alone we are as far as He is concerned. I wonder if that is the reason some folks cannot stand being alone? There is a tug of Somebody that they want to get away from, because they are not fitting into the Law of Abiding.

But when you are alone He is there. And the great thing of the daily quiet place, in the quiet time, is not that you read, though you do read. The Book is as open as the door is shut. It is not that you pray in words, though you will, and you will pray wordlessly. Some of the best prayer is wordless; you cannot get your heart out at your lips.

But the big thing is that He is there, Jesus, by His Holy Spirit, His other self. The Holy Spirit is Jesus' other self; He is inside of every one who opens the door to Jesus. And you sit in His presence, and sing Him a bit of song when you don't want to ask Him for anything, and you thank Him for His presence. Ah, that is the fragrance, that is the power of the quiet time and the quiet place. *Prayer needs a place.*

Then give *the Book its place in prayer.* Prayer is not talking to God simply; it is listen-

ing—listening first, then talking. Bible reading is the listening side of prayer. Some of us
are a little old-fashioned about this Book of
God. Some of us like old-fashioned things,
bread and butter, and salt, and water, and sleep
at night, and—Jesus, and the Blood that
cleanses, and the power within, and the old
Book of God!

They used to burn the Book up. We are
more refined now. We would not burn it.
No; now we cut it up, with rarely-skilled fingers, and freshly-razored knife-edges. But
whether burned or cut the old Book itself re-
mains, without the smell of smoke on its pages,
or the mark of the knife on its leaves.

Now the third bit is this: When you go off
alone in your quiet time, and your quiet place—
listen. God talks. He talked in the Book.
He still talks in it. It is a book like any other
book, yet it is more than a book. There is a
Living Presence in it. Listen to God. Give
Him your ear. It is pathetic what a hard time
God has getting people's ears. The traffic
bothers our ears, and the shuffling of men's
shoes.

What a giant he is who will *take his ears*
away from the crowd, and listen to God! The

ear controls the tongue. If God may have our ears the tongue-part will work all right. If the ear-side of prayer is right, the tongue-side will be right. Give the Book its place. What God says to us through it will absolutely control what we say to Him. Learn to listen with patience.

The fourth suggestion is this: *Let the Teacher teach you.* There is a special Teacher of prayer, One who makes a specialty of teaching how to pray. He is the Holy Spirit, Jesus' Other Self. Where is the Holy Spirit? I carry Him around inside of me. It hushes my heart as I say it. And so do you, if He is given His way. It is not because we are good, but because He is faithful. He comes in through the open door; for it is Jesus' Spirit in us that makes us what we call Christians.

When you go off alone in your quiet time, say, "Lord, teach me." And He will. You may be a bit stupid—most of us are. But He is very patient. You will find your prayer changing. You may be used to making a very nice, proper little speech. I am not criticising it. But now you will find that you pray more simply, you will pray like a child talking with mother, or friend with friend, or partner with partner, where things are understood. Let the Teacher teach you.

And now *the three conditions* of making sure that every prayer will work out a bigger result than you are thinking about: And these are simple but really radical. The first is this: *the controlling purpose of the life to please Jesus.* That may sound very simple. But if you have not done so, take that as a kind of touchstone, testing stone, just for a day, in personal habits, home life, dress, in all things and in a simple, sane, wholesome way.

The thing that *controls* in everything is to please Jesus. Not to ask, " Is it wrong? " and put it out. " Is it right? " and put it in. That is rather a low level. There are many things that are not wrong, but they are not best. Not that, but this: Will it please Jesus?

And, then, if you have the stuff in you to hew to the line of that—ah, there will be a tug —then you will climb the ladder. And you will enter into the secret place where the Law of Abiding controls. And the answer will be bigger than you are expecting. The controlling purpose to please Him.

There is a very striking turn of a word in the end of the second chapter of John. It says a great many believed on Jesus as they listened to Him, but He did not commit Himself to them because He knew all men. If you dig underneath, the word "believe" and the word "commit" are the same. You might read it this way: "A great many trusted Jesus, but He did not trust them because He knew them."

Now, I have no doubt all of us are trusting Him. May I ask you, softly, quietly—Can He trust you? And your eye drops, a tone of humility comes into your voice, and you say: "I fear not." That sounds very nice. But should you say that? If I know a wife well enough to ask such a question, and say, "Can your husband trust you?" she will never answer, "I fear not." If things are as they ought to be, with a hush in her voice and in her eye, she will say quietly, "He knows he has the devotion of my life."

And that sweeps all the decks here. Jesus will give us all the power in prayer He can trust us with to use for His glory. The controlling purpose in everything must be to please Him. If you can stand the tug of that, you will have no bother about the prayer. But it *is* a tug, and it is a tug that does not stop.

The second condition is very old-fashioned.

Your prayer must be *in Jesus' Name.* You and I have no standing at yonder bar, to plead of ourselves. We are debarred, disbarred by sin. We have cut ourselves off. Sin is suicidal. That is rather ugly, but the bother is that it is true, whether you like it or not.

But when we come in Jesus' Name—in the Name of the Man who died on Calvary—it is as though Jesus prayed. It is like this and I want to put it in a very homely way because that helps most: It is as though Jesus said, " Father, here is a friend of Mine from Ohio. We have had an understanding, he and I. We have things fixed up, our law of abiding, and all the ends of the threads are knotted up tight. Please give him anything he asks, for My sake."

And the Father leans over and says: " What will you have? Name it. Anything you choose to name, when My Son talks like this." That is the meaning of using Jesus' Name. We ought to use that Name very thoughtfully, very reverently, very humbly. It cost Him so much pain that we might repeat His name, pain beyond conception. He suffered that we might come and say, " In Jesus' Name."

But we ought to use the name boldly, for

He gives us the right to, when we are in touch with Him. There are many prayers in our day, in church services and prayer-meetings, by men who must be good men, prayers that talk about God, about the Father, but ignore the Name of Jesus. The second condition is that prayer must be *in Jesus' Name*.

The third condition of prayer, again, is very simple, and yet is sometimes not understood. It may sound hackneyed when I say that prayer must be in faith. But faith is not believing that God *can,* it is believing that He *will*—a universe of difference.

Here is what faith is *not*. You kneel, you make your bit of prayer, you say, " In Jesus' Name, Amen." And then you get up from your knees, and say—the thing says itself inside maybe—" I wonder if that will come—I wonder if that will come—I do hope it will." You may have heard your neighbor thinking out loud that way. That is desire, it is intensity, it is yearning, it may be passion; but there is no faith there, of course.

Here is what faith is, in connection with simple prayer: You kneel, you make your bit of prayer, you say: " In Jesus' Name;" and then, when you have got the prayer fixed up, before you tack the "Amen" on, you say, "I thank Thee that Thou art listening, Jesus; I thank Thee that Thou wilt do what I ask, that Thou art doing it; the thing is fixed, although there is a fight ahead—Amen." That is faith.

"Amen" means not "so *may* it be"; but, "so it certainly *shall* be." For "Amen" is not a prayer, it is an affirmation of positive faith. The thing is coming. Then you go off from your knees, around the house, and say to yourself, "That thing is settled. He is coming, it is coming, that is coming." And if you knew that some things you are praying for were coming, would you sing? I think the service of song, in the major key, would flood the house, and threaten the integrity of the roof sometimes. That is faith.

And some dear old saint, or some dear younger saint, will say, "Now, Mr. Gordon, you are getting the music keyed up too high; we cannot sing up in that scale. Bring the thing down where we live. Can we all have faith like that?"

Well, we all *won't* have. That is putting it blunt and honest. We all *may* have, but we all *won't* have. Because the faith that believes that God *will* is not born in a hurry. It is not born in the dust and din and crowd of the street, with the honking of the horns in your ears, and the shuffling of men's shoes.

It never does find a birthplace in some folks' hearts because they won't—they can, but they won't, and they don't—go off alone in the quiet corner with the door shut, and the Book open, and the Somebody there their physical eyes cannot see.

But I will tell you where that faith will be born, and grow big and lusty—in the heart of every one who goes off quietly every day into the quiet place with the Book, and the bent knee and the bent will. Into that heart there will come the quiet assurance that what you are asking He is doing.

Now I think I can tuck in the *four characteristics* of the faith that believes that God *will*. The first characteristic of faith is *intelligence*. It finds out what God's will is. It has listened. When the Holy Spirit has sway the mind is alert. It is not essential to be stupid to be religious. You may have thought it was, from some folks you rub elbows with. When the Holy Spirit has sway there is not simply a new spiritual birth, but a new mental birth.

Faith finds out what God's will is. The Book and the indwelling Spirit make His will clear. The will of God sweeps the whole gamut of human life and need.

The second trait of the faith that knows that God will is *obedience*. The tug of war is here. You keep whipping back here on this bit of truth all the time. Obedience means this. You may find as you are reading the Old Book, and that quiet Spirit is talking to you, you are very apt to find that your life is down here on this lower level, and the Book is up here on the higher level. There are two different levels.

And then the temptation is, by nice religious talk, to pull the Book down to where you want to live. And then all the power goes out of your life. Obedience means this—that by your own set will, and by God's grace, you pull your life up to the level of the Book, in a simple, sane, wholesome way. Nobody is so sane as the man swayed by the Holy Spirit. If you will pull the habit of your life up to the level of the Holy Spirit's voice in the Book, and in your heart, you will have no bother about the rest.

The third trait of faith is *expectancy*. Faith is not blind. It sees the difficulties, but it sees

Jesus greater. It goes to the top of Carmel, and pitches its tent, if need be, and it looks and looks and looks again, for that man to come, for that money to loosen, for that health to come. The faith that believes that God *will* is *expectant*.

And faith is *persistent*. That is the Law of Confidence-Persistence. Prayer is a conflict, a great spirit fight. And there may be a time of waiting. But you *know* that Jesus is Victor and so you go again, seven times, and seventy times seven, and use another multiple of seven if need be; and then you quit counting, and just hang on. And the result comes because Jesus is Victor. The hard heart softens, the stubborn will bends, the hard way straightens, and no thing is restrained.

A little boy of about six came to his mother one day in a Christian home, with Christian training. He said, "Mother, what does it mean to believe on the Lord Jesus?" And the mother quickly recognized that her little boy was beginning to think for himself about the meaning of words that he heard in the home.

And so with a bit of prayer in her heart she said very simply, "Why, you know, my son, it means thinking about Jesus, and thanking Him that He died for you, and loving Him, and telling Him that you will try to please Him in everything you do." And the boy listened, but she could not tell whether he had taken it in.

About an hour later things were suspiciously quiet in the boy's corner of the house: It was not usually so quiet where that boy was. So the mother called, "Charles, where are you? what are you doing?" And as she spoke she was moving over toward the room where he had his toys and books.

And as she came within range of the door, partly open, she saw the boy sitting quietly, with his hands folded on his knees, and his head bent. And the boy, not knowing that his mother was there, called out quietly: "I am believing on the Lord Jesus." He was thinking about Him, loving Him, thanking Him that He died, telling Him he would try to please Him.

Let us *believe* on the Lord Jesus.

Printed in the United States of America